For my children.

~ jf

To all the military daddies who sleep
everywhere when they'd rather be home
with their loved ones. And, to my husband
who knows all too well the pains of sleeping
away from our family.

~tdf

My Daddy Sleeps Everywhere

Text copyright © 2017 by Jesse Franklin

Illustrations copyright © 2017 by Tahna Desmond Fox

ISBN 978-1-938505-25-6 — Paperback. October 2017
ISBN 978-1-938505-26-3 — Hardback. October 2017

Library of Congress Control Number: 2017962226

Printed in the USA ☯ www.lionheartgrouppublishing.com

My Daddy Sleeps Everywhere

Jesse Franklin

Tahna Desmond Fox

Lionheart Group Publishing ❂ www.lionheartgrouppublishing.com
Printed in the USA ❂ Colorado

My daddy sleeps everywhere.
He's not always home.

He sleeps in the forest
where animals roam.

He sleeps in the desert
under star-filled night skies.

He sleeps in the mountains
where bald eagles fly.

He sleeps in the jungle
with vines and big bugs.

8

9

He sleeps on the prairie
where grass keeps him snug.

10

He sleeps on the beach
and waves lull him to sleep.

He sleeps on the rocks
where cacti poke at his feet.

He sleeps in the snow
and he tries to stay warm.

He sleeps in the rain
during big thunderstorms.

He sleeps on airplanes
during long, bumpy flights.

22

He sleeps in the barracks
in faraway places.

He sleeps in broken houses
and tight, dusty spaces.

He sleeps where they tell him
and every night,
he thinks of his family
and tucks in tight.

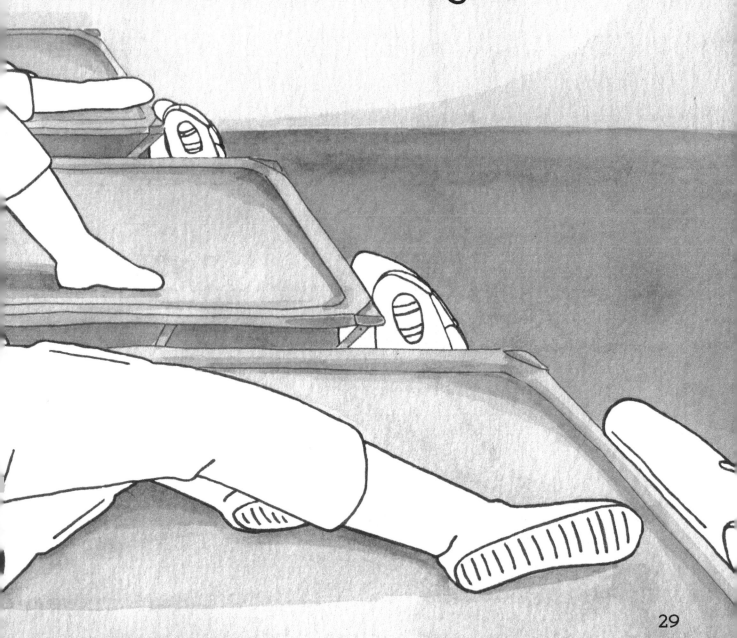

My daddy sleeps everywhere
but everyone knows,
of any place he could sleep
his favorite is home.

JESSE FRANKLIN was raised in the small, high desert town of Green River, Wyoming. He is the father of three wonderful children, husband to a lovely wife, and a United States Marine. His stories are inspired by his family, his experiences in the Marine Corps, and the wonderful people with whom he has served.

TAHNA DESMOND FOX is a formally trained artist who has studied illustration and graphic design for a major portion of her adult life.

Her family is her inspiration, as she continues on her colorful path of illustration and graphic design.

Other Works By This Illustrator

Daddy's Boots

Momma's Boots

But... What If?

Grandpa, What If?

Don't Label Me

Stackable Paige

Oh, My! What Happened?

Sophe's on the Sofa

Squat, The Funny Little Inkblot

What Does a Hero Look Like?

Brooke, and her icky picky sister

My Daddy is a Sailor

Sebastian Earns His Stripes